# Finding Your Voice:

## Rediscover who you are beyond marriage and the challenges of life

## TINA VALIANT

COLEMAN JONES
PRESS

Published in Dallas, Texas by Coleman Jones Press

www.ColemanJonesPress.com

ISBN: 979-8709988675

# Praise for Finding Your Voice

"Finding Your Voice was a game changer for me! Not only did it validate my feelings from losing my identity as a woman within a failed marriage to realizing I was enough and not a victim of my circumstances. I am a survivor who has the power to thrive. Through Tina Valiant's words I also came to the realization that I had not fully forgave my former husband and truly let go. After I did, my world changed forever. It truly is a must read!"

-- *Katie Delnero*, Real Estate Consultant

"I had the very distinct privilege of reading, Finding Your Voice by Tina Valiant, prior to its release. This is a must read book for everyone. The positive impact for women and men will be substantial. It will guide women on how to find their voice and enlighten men on how to help the women in their lives reach their full potential by finding there voice. I highly recommend this book!
-- *Gary L Varnell*, MBA, Best Selling Author and Speaker

"Kudos to Tina Valiant for addressing the elephant in the room for women everywhere! Every woman can identify in some way to the words in this book. Depending on who you listen to for advice, you can be made to feel that you have to choose either your marriage or your dreams. Tina does an incredible job helping people remember who they are, and how to find themselves again, without having to throw away the marriage. She bares her soul on some of the darkest areas of her life and how she got past it all, so that others can feel free to live again. Really great book. *--Tracee Jones*, Author

Finding Your Voice by Tina Valiant, is a book for women of all ages! It offers release, validation, understanding, and affirmation. Being a child of the 60's and 70's, I was encouraged to do my best in all I did. I was always told I was smart and beautiful, but I was also always told that, "Little girls should be seen and not heard!" My dear father meant no harm by that, but it took me 25- 30 years to realize that this philosophy had no place in my adult life.
After I graduated college, gotten married, and began to follow my dreams of being an educator, I truly experienced the "female role" box vs. my dreams that Tina talks about in the book. My first marriage ended because my voice was not heard. I learned that it is NOT selfish to practice self-care in order to be able to help others, and this was a huge relief! I found great truth in the words of Finding Your Voice! As I have aged, I am at peace with having stood up for my self-worth, and expressing my voice, and I encourage you to do the same!

-- Linda O'Neal, Realtor

# CONTENTS

# Introduction

I have met many women who are mothers and wives and are happy with their home life but feel they have a bigger purpose beyond just being a mom and a wife. There are also many women living a life that is controlled by others. If this is you, then this book can help you find your voice. My story is one that explains how I found myself throughout my journey and learned how to practice self-care and self-management by finding my voice. Your journey is not only where you are right now, but also what I call the "dots" of your life that led you to the life you are currently living. Eventually you will be able to connect the dots of your life and this will help you to recognize your gifts and live your purpose.

Writing this book is not only cleansing for me, but it is to inspire those who are stuck in a life that others either control or have chosen for them. At the end of each chapter, you will find a series of questions and exercises for self-reflection that you will be asked to complete. Everything I am asking you to do, I have done myself. Some of the realizations you will discover while reading this book and working through the exercises may be painful, but will help you if you are willing to work through them. Do not read ahead. Don't skip ahead. The purpose they are there is to help you get real with yourself so that you can be real with others.

Always remember that with pain comes growth. Growing is an evolution of yourself and finding your voice through this process. You may uncover some ugly truths about yourself. If so, don't be afraid to work through them. We all have ugly truths. You will recognize how much you are suppressing yourself and why you feel unsettled inside. If I accomplish my goal, you may even uncover some repressed goals and dreams that you have tucked away and forgotten about.

In speaking to men and women why there are so many unsettled marriages and divorce, there is a direct correlation. Women tend to suppress themselves after marriage. Men tend to miss the women they married because their wives put themselves into a box, filling a role they have been taught since birth. They lose who they are -- their goals, ambitions, and confidence --for what they believe to be the greater good of the family, when in most cases their husband didn't ask them to go into this box!

It is important for me to share with you where I came from so that you can understand how I came to the knowledge and life of a survivor. This book is filled with lessons I have learned on my journey as well as stories of other triumphant women. What I have found throughout my life and through my conversations with other women is that we are resilient. Given the right tools, we have the ability to overcome all obstacles! We have the ability to thrive against all odds of adversity. I hope you will grow as you go through this process with me. I am not an educated psychologist, nor did I believe years ago that I would be writing a book for women.

As you go through this book, you will uncover why you repressed your voice and regain who you are again! This is not a book promoting women's liberation. I believe women need men just as much as men need women! There is a way to co-exist and be who you are, a woman with a voice, dreams, who had plans and goals before you married,. Take this journey with me and so many other women who are just like you! Dare to dream of becoming your authentic self and feeling fulfilled in all aspects of your life! Regain who you are because you are worth it and you were made for greatness!

# CHAPTER ONE

# My Story

I grew up in a tumultuous childhood filled with every abuse imaginable at the hand of different men in my life. I lived in an unsafe world where I was at the mercy of others and they were not kind to me. As a child, I accepted that this was how others lived and accepted it as being no different than anybody else.

My parents were married at a very young age and divorced by the time I was two years old. My father took a traveling job after the divorce because not having me full time killed him deep inside. I wouldn't understand his choices until much later in life. My mother loved me dearly but was a struggling young mother who worked around the clock to ensure our survival. I was taken care of by family where my mother thought I would be safe. Nobody knew the abuse I was suffering at the hand of my much older cousin. I was four years old when he began molesting me. The molestation continued until I was seven years old.

My mother married a man that she thought would be a good father for me when I was six. Looking back, prior to

1

their marriage, he seemed he would be. He was a fun and kind man to me at first, but from the moment they married his actions towards me changed. He became mentally and physically abusive. I was beaten almost daily and told horrible things like, "Nobody could ever love you," "you are so ugly," and "you will never amount to anything in life." As a child, I believed him.

He always looked so big to me. Later in life, I ran into him and he seemed so small compared to how he had appeared to me when I was a child. He seemed so powerless. It is funny how your perspective is so different as a child. This went on until I was eleven, when my mother finally decided she wanted a divorce. I was elated to say the least but there were other problems to follow.

My mother had become an addict while married to him and after the divorce I was alone most of the time. I was fighting at school regularly and had such rage inside. I was angry at the world for the life I had been given! I used my fists to pummel other kids in hopes I would feel better, but I didn't. The rage continued to build up inside and if things hadn't changed, I don't know where I would be today.

After my twelfth birthday, my mother decided she wanted to get better. We moved to Colorado to live with her best friend whom I called my aunt. My mom slept for weeks on end as she recovered from her addictions. I didn't know at the time why she was so sick. I thought she was just sad because we left her friends, boyfriend, and family, behind as well as my little brother. She continued to fight and get better until we could live on our own. This was my first experience seeing her fight and triumph as my mother became herself again. Her determination became an inspiration to me.

Shortly after we moved into our own apartment, my mom's boyfriend moved to our town and into our apartment with us. He was a good man who wanted to provide for us and keep us safe. Needless to say, life was better with him in it. He later became my step-father and who I still call "Dad" today. He was the first example in my life of a man who lived his true purpose to provide and protect. Between him and my aunt, my mother, my brother, and I were safe and could begin to grow.

Still, I did not understand why I was so angry inside. My life was better but there were still unresolved problems at home. My mother and I fought continuously. Looking back, I realize it was because I didn't trust the feeling of being safe. Because of the many years that I endured mental, physical, and sexual abuse, I didn't know how to have friends or trust anybody. I went through many years unable to form real relationships with people.

One day, a neighbor of mine asked me to go to youth group with her at church. I was hesitant at first, but decided to go and take a look. Everybody was so friendly and smiling. They sang worship songs and cried with joy. The pastor, I will never forget his name, Barney Huie, spoke with such passion as he jumped all over the stage.

He gave a message on love and hope. By the end, he had an altar call and I was moved to go forward. Pastor Huie laid his hands on me and I just started sobbing. My body convulsed as all of the anger and pain drained out of me. I didn't know this feeling or understand what was happening. All I knew was I needed this love and hope this man spoke about! I was broken into a million pieces, and for the first time in my life, it was okay.

After youth group, I went home and everything looked different to me. Even my parents looked different. For the first time, I could see them as human and understood that they were broken as well. I could feel their pain. The only way I can explain it now is that an enlightenment awoke inside me. Everything I believed fell away and I could see who we were all meant to be.

I continued going to church by myself about three or four times per week. All I knew was I felt accepted there. I had a love of singing and began singing in the choir, as well as singing solos during church services.

I joined the drama team and began acting in church plays and monologues. My parents, although they were convinced I had joined a cult, could not deny the changes in me. They started going to church on occasion to hear me sing. Eventually they joined the church as well and dedicated their lives to God. Our family, as a whole, began to mend and heal.

Now I must take a moment to explain a couple of things. My life and what I experienced at a young age had devastating consequences. All humans need to feel safe and secure. I found my safety and security through forming a relationship with God. Church was the conduit that helped me get there, but the relationship was with God. When I opened myself to God's love and acceptance of me, something profound happened. I was gifted with an enlightenment and an understanding of others around me and things to come. In Christian circles, this gift of enlightenment is referred to as the gift of the Holy Spirit. My gift has grown over the years as I have embraced it and understand its purpose for the greater good of humanity.

However, my brokenness did not disappear and has been an evolution of my learning to love myself and forgive those that have hurt me. There have been many choices that have had consequences in the life that I have chosen. My desire for the feeling of safety and security have taken me down many roads of broken promises and heartbreak because I was looking outwardly for what must come from within. My first marriage is a perfect depiction of what I mean.

I married very young into a wealthy family. They lived a life I had only dreamt about. I was always provided for and had everything I could possibly want materialistically. We always had nice homes, new cars, and new clothes. I gave birth to two beautiful daughters in our first few years of marriage. Outwardly everything looked perfect.

Behind closed doors the actual picture was that I was suffocating. I wasn't allowed to have an opinion about anything. I wasn't allowed to choose my clothes, wear high heels, change my jewelry, carry a checkbook or a credit card, or have friends. I lived in a world where from the moment my husband got home from work at 2:30 in the afternoon, all blinds were closed, nobody was allowed to call, and I was at his mercy for the rest of the evening. Have you ever seen the movie Sleeping with the Enemy? That was my life without the physical abuse.

I survived this world for twelve years and then moved to Florida. I had lost my voice and fought desperately to regain it. I will tell you more about my defining moment, which changed everything, in the next chapter.

As I think back on it, my story is not unlike so many that I meet regularly. I consider myself a survivor but also one that has learned how to thrive amid adversity. My goals, my drive, and my vision have grown over time and have brought me to a place where I can share my knowledge and what I have learned with you so that you can also find your voice and learn to thrive in this world.

CHAPTER TWO

# Defining Moments

W hat is a defining moment in your life? I can tell
you I have had at least two, very direct in-my-face
moments that changed my life forever. I call them
"defining moments" because life could not and would not
be the same after they happened. I could never be the same.

I shared my story of my first marriage with you. I
briefly mentioned a change in my mindset that then led to
a change in me. It was the first defining moment in my life;
my first realization that I was not happy with my life. It was
the moment that began to set the stage for who I am today.

I was living in Colorado with my husband and two
daughters. My girls were both in school, my husband was
working and seemed fine. I was working at this charming
Day Spa about 30 hours a week. One of the other therapists I
worked with came to me and explained there was something
unique about me. After some exploration we discovered that
I had natural healing hands, which was so exciting to me. On
the outside, everything appeared amazing. Nobody knew

the extreme pain emotionally I was in, but they also didn't know the physical pain I was experiencing consistently.

For years I had been plagued with abdominal pain. It had gone undiagnosed for quite some time and continued to get worse. By the age of 27, the doctors were so perplexed by my symptoms. They swore up and down it must be female related, and they needed to conduct an exploratory surgery. At that point I did not care what they needed to do as long as they could figure out what the debilitating pain was that was stabbing the right side of my stomach constantly!

During the surgery, the doctors decided to take my appendix. While exploring inside, they found a wall of scar tissue across my lower abdominal wall that was completely unexplained. There were cysts on my ovaries, especially the right side. Basically, I was a mess but there was no explanation as to the cause. Quite frankly, they didn't know. The "process of elimination" surgeries (as I called them), started the following month and lasted for the next two years. My pain continued to intensify, and I had to spend more and more time in bed.

The doctors were so quick to prescribe pain medicine after pain medicine. I would try one or two, they wouldn't work, and I would put the entire bottle into a grocery bag full of bottles and make another appointment. At one point, I got flagged at the pharmacy for being a "pill head".

I took the bag of painkillers and anti-inflammatories back to the pharmacist to show him I still had them all. I then took them all to my doctor and basically gave them all back! The doctors offered me antidepressants and my response was; "Why would I need those? Is it new that antidepressants take away severe abdominal pain?" I was extremely frustrated to say the least, and I think the doctors were as well. I had to keep reminding myself that it is the "practice" of medicine not the "knowledge" of medicine.

By the time I was 29 years old, both of my ovaries had been removed, as well as my uterus, appendix, and possibly other things. I had spent two years pretty much in bed, in pain, fighting with doctors, fighting with my husband, and barely able to keep my job. I was exhausted! I felt worse about my two young daughters not having an energetic and healthy mommy.

I believed with the last surgery we had finally found the problem. To my utter and complete horror, the pain returned and with a vengeance. I could not eat or drink anything, not even water. The pain was so excruciating. I couldn't walk, sit, lay down, or even breathe without stabbing pain piercing my stomach from every direction. After two straight days of getting worse, I finally told my husband I needed to go to the doctor or the ER. The ER doctors took one look at me -- my pale skin, frail body, high fevers, shivering uncontrollably from pain -- and checked me in immediately as a high priority.

For three days, I underwent test upon test upon test. After my initial bloodwork the doctors came into my room

# Defining Moments

(several of them), and this became, right here, the defining moment where neither I nor my life could ever be the same. "Tina, your blood work is all over the place and not good. We are so sorry to say this, but we believe you have cancer and we believe it is advanced. We are trying to find it. Tina, you are very sick and may not make it out of this hospital bed. Is there anybody we need to call for you?"

Let me break this down for you. I am 29 years old, I have two beautiful young daughters that I had not created enough memories with. I remember looking across the room that day at my husband and thinking "I don't even like you as a person. I haven't for a long time." My thoughts drifted to all of my lost hopes and dreams, all the things I wanted to do; places I wanted to go. My life could just be over like that? I didn't have enough time, or maybe I had time but didn't utilize it well? All I knew for sure was if I ever made it out of that hospital bed my life had to change. It became so clear that I wanted more! I knew in that defining moment, I had a new direction and passion for life! My new motto became "live life with no regrets because you never know what day will be your last."

My second defining moment was more recent and almost an identical story. God is funny when he wants your attention and needs to remind you of the previous lessons you learned -- but didn't remember. My abdominal pain had resurfaced and kept increasing for several days. I called my best friend and personal assistant to take me to the ER.

10

This time they admitted me right away because I had a severe infection in my colon due to a perforation, and the infection began to move through my body. My white blood cell count was all over the place and had I waited just one more day, the doctors said they may not have been able to save me. I would have died. After four days of intense treatments, I was released from the hospital with a date scheduled to remove a portion of my large intestines. The diagnosis was different. However, the message was the same: *"Live life with no regrets because you never know when today could be your last."*

Unfortunately, the infection would not go away despite taking several different antibiotics throughout a months' time. The doctors were trying to give my colon time to heal prior to having a bowel resection. Their efforts were to no avail and I spent over a month at home; very ill, awaiting the surgery. A surgery that was supposed to last one hour and be minimally invasive ended up lasting three hours; with a five-inch incision. My small intestines were looped to my large intestines because of an abscess created by one of the two perforations. The surgeon informed me that my life was on the line the entire month I had been home, and my body was being poisoned by my perforations. He said I was lucky to be alive and I must say I agree with him! Clearly, my work on this earth was not done!

I can assure you I will not forget the lessons I have learned moving forward. Live life with no regrets. Live a life with purpose and meaning. Make sure every person that you love knows you love them. Treat every moment as if it could be your last breath and savor it with all of you. You never know when it will be your last.

# For Reflection

Have you had a defining moment that in essence "woke you up?" Write down your experience.

_____

_____

_____

_____

_____

What happened that caused your defining moment and what did you realize about yourself and your life?

_____

_____

_____

_____

_____

How would you like for things to be different?

_____

_____

_____

_____

_____

_____

The most difficult part of this exercise is getting real with yourself. It was difficult for me to admit I wasn't the mom I wanted to be and that I didn't like my husband as a person. Somewhere inside, I believed if I didn't say it or write it, the feelings either didn't exist or would go away. The reality is that if we don't identify the feelings, they continue to grow inside of us, creating a hole in our heart that can't be filled.

Maybe reading this chapter is a defining moment for you, and the words have opened your eyes to feelings deep down inside. Count your blessings, if that is the case, because it means you don't have to be brought to a place of physical pain or loss to open yourself. I encourage you to go through the exercise and uncover your inner hidden feelings that you don't articulate to anybody because of fear of what might happen. This chapter is a pivotal point in your growth throughout this book. You cannot unlock your voice if you cannot be real with yourself. If you need to take some time and really ponder this part of the process, please do so. Once you have completed the exercise, you are ready to move forward.

# CHAPTER THREE

# The Underdog

As you have read in "Defining Moments", I realized I needed to make changes in my life. Not just changes on the outside. I needed to make changes on the inside as well. As you begin to make changes in your personal life, your entire world begins to open up and the possibilities become endless.

After my first husband and I moved to Florida, and I began receiving treatment for Crohns disease, I began to heal physically from my illness. I knew that I needed a career where I would be able to support my daughters and I financially. Friends of mine from church knew my desire to look for employment and thought I should interview for a position in timeshare sales. My friend's husband was making a six-figure income and doing very well for his family in the business. He felt I had what it took to make the same income as him. He set up an interview for me with his sales manager at the resort. I was apprehensive to say the least because this was a huge opportunity for me!

The day of the interview, I had to borrow clothes from my friend. I had been a stay-at-home mom for quite some time and did not have the professional wardrobe I would need for the position. My friend assured me that she would help me put some things together if I were hired. As I was driving to the interview, I prayed that if this was the plan the Lord had for me, he would open the doors. I was shaking like crazy when I exited my car and entered the resort. There were salespeople fluttering around, dressed beyond professional and downright classy. I remember looking down at myself and thinking there was no way I would fit in here. I kept asking the Lord if I was worthy of this career.

As I interviewed with the Sales Manager, I felt as if someone was answering the questions for me. I couldn't tell you to this day what questions were asked other than one. "If somebody lies to you, what do you do?" My answer was, "ask them the question in a different way until you get the truth." At the end of the interview, the Sales Manager shook my hand and welcomed me to the team.

The training class would begin in two weeks and I had to have my real estate licensing class finished prior to attending training. He warned me that training would be very intense for three weeks and if I wasn't able to keep up or memorize everything, I would never make it to the sales floor.

As I left the resort, my heart was pounding out of my chest. I could not believe what just happened! Me, a housewife --- borrowing clothes from my friend to attend the interview -- being offered a career in potentially a six figure per year position? The negative thoughts of myself began to rise in my mind. Was I worthy of this? Would I fail? Could I meet their expectations of me? Could I meet the expectations of myself?

I prayed for the Lord to give me a sign that I was supposed to continue on this journey. If I was able to get into real estate class and complete it prior to my training class beginning, I would accept that this is what God wanted for me. Low and behold, the third real estate school I called, made an exception for me and allowed me to begin class the next day. My class would be completed within ten days, just in time for me to begin my training class. It was clear I was meant to move forward.

Training was more intense than anything I had ever experienced. Each long day was filled with memorizing a 50-page script, product knowledge, and sales techniques. At the end of training, I was warned that I would be tested on all of the materials and would have to write and say aloud the 50-page script. If I missed anything on the test or one word in the script, I would be fired! Every day for three weeks, I went home after class and studied until bedtime.

My husband was not thrilled with my new career and intentionally tried to sabotage me nightly. His sabotage attempts became so terrible that I had to lock myself in the guest room and move furniture in front of the door so that he could not get into the room. To make it worse, my classmates voted me least likely to succeed out of the class because I did not have the "look" or the sales knowledge the rest of them had. I held on to faith that the Lord had opened the door for me to have that position, and I was going to succeed!

I passed my training tests with flying colors and made it to the sales floor. I only had ten opportunities to make a sale or I would be fired. There was no way in the world I was going to let that happen after all I went through to get here. While on the sales floor, one of my female managers came to me and asked me to go home and change my clothes because I was not dressed well enough to be on the sales floor. I was so ashamed and embarrassed. I drove directly to Ross and bought five dresses that I could rotate each week. My husband was so angry that I spent $80.00 on dresses but I did not care. I showed up the next day with a new dress on and my female manager smiled when she saw me. She nodded in approval and went on about her day.

The other salespeople sat in the backroom playing cards and hanging out with each other. I sat in the corner listening to sales CDs. They all thought I was stuck up because I didn't fraternize with them. They didn't realize this career meant my freedom and there was nothing that was going to stand in my way. After every presentation with guests, I would ask my closing managers what I needed to do differently. I would sit for hours picking their brain so that I could improve my skills. By my seventh presentation, I had success. My guests purchased!

My eighth presentation purchased as well. I became a three in ten closer, which in the timeshare world is superstar status. By the end of the second month on the sales floor, I had made it to the top ten percent of the resort out of 268 agents and maintained my status throughout my career. Nobody from my original training class was left at the resort after the first two months. I was the only one out of eleven that had made it.

I have been the underdog many times in my life and have learned that this is where I thrive. While in Florida, many of my friends and colleagues told me I would be terrible in residential real estate. They said I didn't have the patience and couldn't learn everything I needed to know to be successful. I had developed a reputation as the shortsale negotiator – from where I started helping people who were about to have their homes foreclosed on, and I just could not get people to see me in a different light. By the time I moved to Arizona in 2016, I had my real estate license for over sixteen years.

For the first few months I was there, I tried putting my efforts into other things besides Real Estate. I didn't have a savings built up and knew that going back into a commission only industry would take some time to start getting paid. I finally bit the bullet in January of 2017 when I had a continually nagging feeling inside that I was meant to activate my license.

For the first few days after activating my real estate license,

I realized I was holding on to a lot of hurt and past betrayal from others that I needed to let go of. Most people do not realize how much your past can affect your performance in business. I was paralyzed because of things that had occurred over the years and I was riddled with fear of the unknown. After several days of journaling, which we'll discuss in more detail in the chapter on forgiveness, I was ready to hit the ground running.

Because so many people had told me I would never be good at residential real estate, I was afraid I was going to fall flat on my face. I began with conducting open houses and had to make a paycheck in six weeks or my family was not going to have a place to live. I found myself in a position of walking purely in faith once again. I had to believe this was the direction I was supposed to go in and because of my faith, everything was going to work out.

The second weekend conducting open houses, I sold the home I was holding open to a cash buyer! We closed the day before all of my bills were due. After the first contract was written, I did not stop! I kept pushing myself and momentum continued building. People started coming to me asking to join my team. I thought to myself, "well, I guess I am going to be a team leader." My first year selling real estate in Arizona, I sold forty-two homes and was nominated Rookie of the Year for the entire state by the Arizona Business Journal.

I started creating training materials for my team members

on corporate level sales training. My team started winning awards year one for sales and volume! I developed the trainings further and created workshops for other real estate agents from all over the country. Amazingly, the people that once told me I would not succeed in real estate are people today that ask to attend my workshops.

When you have faith and determination, anything is possible. It takes putting in the work from the inside out. You must search within yourself for what is holding you back. Why are there limiting beliefs clouding your mind? You are capable of anything you set your mind to as long as you believe you can.

Your greatest enemy is not those around you. Your greatest enemy is yourself. You must begin the work to free your mind and your spirit. You must let go of past pain and learn to forgive those that have hurt you. You must recognize the lies that have been spoken over your life for exactly what they are...lies! It is time for you to become free to be exactly who you are meant to be! There is no greater victory than an underdog winning the race!

CHAPTER FOUR

# *Who Are You Inside?*

T he question of who we are inside can be frightening and exhilarating all at the same time. We, as women, tend to put who we are aside for the greater good of those around us. We make sacrifices and tend to put our dreams and total being on hold to avoid conflict and nurture those around us. We become chameleons to our circumstances, changing our colors with each situation to ensure peace. We lose who we really are over time as we continue to suffocate the voice within ourselves.

In a previous chapter, I asked you to identify how you really feel about your life. It may have brought pain to you, but without pain, we cannot grow. We must first open the wounds in order to feel them properly. Now that the wounds of repression and emptiness are open, let's look at how we begin to heal so that we can be the best version of ourselves!

The questions I want you to ask yourself are: How did you get to a point of losing who you are? Did you settle in life? Did you give up who you were for a life you believed would fill a void in you? Before you can find your voice, you must first identify who you really are and what you want out of life. In this chapter, we will explore what your original goals and dreams were before you repressed them. One of the many common denominators in women I mentor is that overwhelming realization that they gave up who they were to have the life they have now.

As little girls, we are filled with the idea of "happily ever after". The prince rides in on his white horse and saves the princess from evil. They ride off into the sunset to their happily ever after. We are taught that your goal should be a grandiose wedding, having children, taking care of your home, and pleasing your husband. Does this sound familiar?

In this picture that has been created since birth, the female leaves her family, friends, and gives up her dreams because the main focus is on getting married and being "saved by her prince." Marriage is where she will find her safety and security. Marriage will create her happily ever after. Nobody actually tells us how hard marriage is or that happily ever after actually exists for very few people. But why does it have to be very few people? Why can't it be the majority? We go into marriage and relationships with pre-determined expectations and begin putting ourselves into a box we believe we are supposed to be in to have our fairytale lifestyle.

The box I am referring to is the "female role" box just as men have their "male role" box. The females' box looks something like this: From the time you are married, you are to keep the peace by doing all things that are expected of you. You should give up your dreams and goals in order to be supportive of your husband. You should take care of the house, have children and take care of them, create a place of peace for your family, and in this day and age, work a full-time job while maybe only sleeping five or so hours a night! I don't know about you, but this sounds like an exhausting life, not to mention the fact you are also expected to stay fit, eat healthy, look beautiful...the list goes on and on!

Men put themselves into a box of provider and protector. We do not realize how much pressure they put on themselves to bring home enough money, protect their family, keep their wife happy and help with any problem that may arise. Just like we women, because of their duty as a husband, they may have left their goals and dreams aside as well. Many husbands have shared with me that their main focus is for their wife to be happy. They come to me perplexed on where the woman they married went. These conversations helped me realize we have an epidemic of women forgetting who they are inside and then becoming really angry with themselves, and their husband or significant other because of it!

I was recently talking to a guy we'll call Sam, a husband in his thirties who has a glowing career, beautiful kids, and a gorgeous wife. On the outside Sam appeared happy and seemed like he had a poster worthy family. We started talking about my concept for this book and his eyes lit up as he asked if I could help his wife. I was actually taken aback with his question as total fear and concern rolled across his face.

I began asking Sam questions about his wife. Sam started telling me about who she was when they met. He said she was vivacious and so full of life. Her beauty on the inside as well as the outside was astounding to him. He was attracted to her ambition and zest for life. They joked all the time and had fun together. These qualities are what drew him to her. He knew without question this was the woman he wanted by his side in life and in love. Sam's depiction of his wife was beautifully magnificent but there was a key word as he described her. He specifically used the word "was."

As I began asking him questions about what had changed, sadness rolled across his face. Sam said his wife had become insecure, nagging, and seemed to constantly be mad at him, but he wasn't sure why. I knew immediately that his wife was not fulfilling her original goals and dreams. She put her vision aside to have the children and maintain her life and home. As soon as they were married, she became pregnant and put herself into the box of who she thought she was supposed to be.

As Sam shared this part of the story with me, I could feel his sadness and almost heartbreak. He expressed the struggle at home as, what I would call, his wife fighting to get herself back. Sam's biggest concern was how to show support towards his wife finding herself again in hopes the woman he chose and married would come back to him.

He expressed how much he missed her and loved her with everything in him. Sam was scared to death he would lose his wife because she felt it was his fault that she lost herself along the way, thus the anger she was expressing towards him. Sam shared that he never wanted his wife to give up anything she wanted to do, as her ambition was one of the many things he loved about her. His desire was to help her find herself again.

The key to this story -- and so many others that I hear; Sam never asked his wife to put herself in the box. She did it on her own because that is what women are taught from a young age. Sam loved that she was confident and secure. These are common statements from husbands around the globe! They want to know why their wives changed because they did not ask them to. They loved who their wives were.

Do you find yourself repressed and having feelings of wanting to crawl out of your skin? I have felt that way a few times in my life. As I reflected on my own life over the past several years, I realized I had put myself into the box of who I thought I was supposed to be in my role as a wife and mother. How do we stop the insanity of putting ourselves into this box that isn't what we want? We must first identify who we are inside and then make a promise to ourselves and our loved ones to never let that person inside of us go!

Working through the questions at the end of this chapter is key to helping you find you again. Maybe you lost yourself because of pain or betrayal. Maybe you lost yourself because you too put yourself into this "fairytale box" and started playing the role of who you thought you were supposed to be. These are all limiting beliefs that have been created in your mind that are forcing you to suppress who you really are inside. You must do the work to find you again. You must reach deep inside to recover what you have lost. In doing so, you will begin to find your voice again. It is time to reclaim who you are!

# *For Reflection*

How do you feel today?

_____

_____

_____

_____

Are you missing something that was once important to you but that you put aside?

_____

_____

_____

_____

Write down a list of characteristics you feel you have lost along the way.

_____

_____

_____

Do you feel a hole in your life, almost like there is an emptiness?

_____

_____

_____

_____

What is it that you believe is causing you to feel this way?

_____

_____

_____

Do you feel repressed in your voice?

_____

_____

_____

_____

Is your repression because you have chosen to repress your thoughts and feelings or is there somebody in your life not allowing you to express yourself?

_____

_____

_____

_____

In the space below, write down all the thoughts and feelings that you have about different things in your life and get real with yourself. This is for you and nobody else. Drop the fear and be honest!

_____

_____

_____

_____

_____

_____

What were your goals and dreams growing up?

_____
_____
_____
_____
_____
_____
_____
_____
_____
_____
_____
_____

Did you take steps to fulfill them?

_____
_____
_____
_____

If you fulfilled them, have you maintained your goals and dreams?

**YES**          **NO**          **SOME**

☐               ☐               ☐

## Goal or Dream                    Accomplished          Set Aside

_____ ☐ ☐

_____ ☐ ☐

_____ ☐ ☐

_____ ☐ ☐

_____ ☐ ☐

_____ ☐ ☐

_____ ☐ ☐

_____ ☐ ☐

_____ ☐ ☐

_____ ☐ ☐

_____ ☐ ☐

_____ ☐ ☐

_____ ☐ ☐

_____ ☐ ☐

_____ ☐ ☐

_____ ☐

What did you sacrifice within you to have the life you have now?

_____
_____
_____
_____

Can you identify why you gave those things up? Was it you or did somebody ask you to give them up?

_____
_____
_____
_____

Write down what you have sacrificed and who, if anyone, asked you to give them up. Really think about if it was your choice or somebody else's request of you. If it was somebody else, why did you agree to their request? What was your fear if you didn't honor their request?

_____
_____
_____
_____
_____
_____
_____
_____
_____
_____
_____

_____

_____

_____

_____

_____

_____

_____

_____

_____

_____

_____

_____

Are you satisfied with how things have turned out in your life?

_____

Is there anything that you would like to change about your life that you feel is holding you back as a person or preventing you from having the satisfaction out of life you deserve? Write a list of things you are satisfied with and a list of things you are not satisfied with in your life.

# *Satisfied*

# Not Satisfied

Are you ready for your next chapter to be different? Why can't you have it all? Looking at your life now, is it possible to move things around to begin this new chapter in your life? Look at your calendar and determine how much you do for others as opposed to how much you do for yourself. Start adding things to your calendar daily that are just for you.

Let's begin the changes to move forward with who you want to be. Looking at the next ten years of your life, what do you want that ten years to look like? Make a list of how you feel you can accomplish your ten-year goal. This can be scary because it may mean you need to make some significant changes. Do not be afraid! Each change you make will bring another change. Look at it as climbing a mountain. If you look to the top of the mountain, you may never begin the journey because it looks too high and scary. The best way to climb a mountain is to take one step at a time, never looking down or to the top. Just keeping focus on one step at a time. In no time, you will be at the top of the mountain, thankful that you made it! Life can be tackled just like climbing a mountain. Think of the smallest changes you can make to begin this journey and then take the first step. Write them here.

_____

_____

_____

_____

CHAPTER FIVE

# *You Are Enough*

Feelings of inadequacy have plagued our society. Everywhere we turn there are pictures of what we as "ideal women" are supposed to look like. As we turn on the television or watch movies, we are again reminded of how inadequate we are, not only in appearance but also in intelligence, wit, and career. Pornography has reached an all-time high because of the instant gratification of free online porn sites that offer unrealistic expectations and depictions of not only how the ideal sex symbol should look but also unrealistic acts of sexual encounters. If we are single, online dating is no better! First, we must look the part only to be ousted by the next shiny object to give instant gratification and validation of desire. How do we compete with any of this?

We don't! We take a stand of acceptance of ourselves for who we are: Real women, exactly as we look, as we act, and owning our desires. We are enough just as we are! We should walk in confidence of who we are and stop comparing ourselves to unrealistic images that have riddled through our minds.

It might come as a surprise to you, but many men have shared with me on numerous occasions that they love women who have curves. They love women to look real and not made up with tons of makeup. They love women who are confident, secure, and own who they are. Men do not care about a few extra pounds, how perfect you look, or whether you have stretch marks or scars. They desire a woman who walks in confidence and loves herself. Of course, I am speaking about the majority of men. The reality is, if all those other things are at the top of a man's list, he is probably not the man you want anyway!

Being enough is not just about what we look like, our career, how sassy we are in the bedroom, or any of the outward appearances people see. It is more about how we feel about ourselves inside. In the last chapters, I asked you to start realizing who you are inside. Recognizing who you really are is the first step in embracing who you are; thus finding love for yourself. Many years ago, I realized that people are going to either love or dislike me. I gained an acceptance that I could not control how others felt about me, but I could control loving myself and being true to me. The most amazing thing happened once I stopped caring what others thought. More people ended up liking me because I was being my authentic self. They were drawn to me because I was real in a world filled with fake people.

Do you see those people on social media that give off the perception that everything is so perfect in their lives? You know the ones. They have perfect teeth, hair, smile, living exotic lives and love posting about how absolutely amazing everything is in their life, love, and business? I call this the "fake perception" because it makes them feel validated. I decided long ago I would rather be real and not give off a fake perception of myself! Now, don't get me wrong. It is better to be positive on social media. I'm not saying to be gloom and doom, my world is ending. I am saying it is OK to show some vulnerability and real feelings.

It's like being at the grocery store and seeing somebody you know. They always ask how you have been, and our mind tells us they are not being genuine in their question. Our conscience goes to "Do they really care or are they just being polite? Should I say everything is amazing and just move on?" We don't give this thought process a second thought but why? What if we were honest in that moment by saying "Most things have been going great, just a few hiccups here and there, but that is life." Now that is an authentic and real statement! Not being honest in most cases is because we are afraid of others response; therefore we just pass through life feeling inadequate, unworthy, and not enough!

*Do you feel you are enough?* I want you to dive deep in this moment and ask yourself if you believe you are enough.

Most of our self-sabotage and negative self-talk is because of our deep-seeded belief that we are not worthy of more. I want to share with you a story that illustrates one of the most meaningful transformations I've ever witnessed in all the people I've mentored and coached. We'll call this person Maria.

Maria had a loving and kind husband. Her two children were beautiful, happy, and healthy. Her husband was a great provider, and she had everything she could need or want materialistically. Maria found herself wanting more out of her life personally. She felt such guilt for not being able to be content with her blessings. Maria had a desire to somehow be a contribution to others beyond her home and family. She knew she needed something she could call her own, but what?

Maria and her husband brainstormed about different ideas of launching a career for her. Her husband was completely supportive of Maria making her mark! Together, they decided on Real Estate. When Maria first came to me, she was very frustrated. She had gotten her Real Estate license, went to all of the training classes she could find, and was doing everything her instructors told her to do to be successful. After several months, she had one sale under her belt, which was her own house. She was determined she was going to figure out the real estate world.

I took her with me to show property one day. I felt it would give she and I time to figure out what was really going on with her, and boy did it! I took one look at Maria before we loaded the car for the day and thought to myself, "What in the world is she wearing?" She had on a crazy looking denim skirt with a flower pattern in the seams, a flowered blouse that did not match the pattern on the skirt, and black tennis shoes. She also had on this little lacy hat that she had made. It was hard for me not to be embarrassed when I introduced her to my clients. The other, most important item, she had with her was a notebook. Maria wrote down every word I said all day!

After the showings were complete, we had an hour-long drive home. I asked her what she really wanted out of this career? Maria's response was priceless. "I want to make people happy. I want to help them. I want to be a contribution!" Maria was emphatic about her desire! She explained that she wanted to create success for herself, but she didn't know how. She also explained her frustration in not understanding why it wasn't working.

She had passion inside her like few people I had ever met. She was dedicated to her pursuit. I decided in that moment, we needed to have a tough conversation and get real. I hesitated but cared for Maria and her success. I looked at her with seriousness yet compassion and began, "Maria, if you are serious about this career, and I believe you are, I need to have a tough conversation with you."

She pulled out her trusty notebook to take notes as I spoke. "Maria, people suck! It's not fair but they do. Unfortunately, their perception becomes your reality." She looked at me wide-eyed and gave me a nod of acceptance. I paused, sad to have to say my next words, trying to be as delicate as possible. "If you and I went up against each other for a listing, based on appearance alone, not because I am the most beautiful woman in the world, but because I am well put together, who would the client choose?"

She looked at me without hesitation as she answered, "They would choose you." I could feel her defeat as she answered. My response surprised her, "If you know that to be the answer then why are you self-sabotaging yourself?" The tears started to flow as she answered, "I don't know. It's just something that I do. I don't know how to stop or where to even begin." I was so proud of her for getting real with herself and me in that moment! She completely dropped her guard and showed a vulnerable sweet spirit that needed help. This woman right before me, I could work with!

I came up with a plan that would have to be agreed upon before she joined my team. Maria needed a makeover and I would help her. It took Maria two weeks to give a firm commitment. Her husband was completely on board and gave her an open budget to spend whatever she needed. Those that know me know that I dislike shopping, but this woman was worth the three-hour shopping trip it took to find her the right clothing for her career. I found out some very important things while we spent time together. She wore tennis shoes because she had surgery on both of her ankles which caused her to need extra support, so we chose shoes online that would help her feel pretty. As I was picking clothes for her, she began to smile bigger. She went home and tried on all of the clothes in her closet, sending me pictures for the "yes" and "no" piles. She donated everything that was a "no".

On the day of her hair appointment, she had a cut and color and was so excited as she wore one of her new outfits! I had her meet me at the office to show me her new look. I wanted her to see and feel the reactions of others in the office. She had no idea that was my goal. She walked in and the first person to see Maria was the receptionist. She took one look at Maria and tears welled up in her eyes as she ran around the desk to hug Maria. She couldn't believe the transformation! One by one as people saw Maria, they gave her hugs and congratulated her on her new, professional look. Maria didn't know how to respond but I felt her inner glow start to rise.

After we went outside, I turned to her and asked her how she felt. Her response made me freeze for a moment, "I didn't realize how much I needed a makeover. I didn't realize how people saw me before. Why did you do this for me? Why was it important to you to help me in this way?" I realized in that moment that we had a much bigger obstacle to overcome. Maria did not feel she was enough. She didn't feel worthy of others seeing her beauty on the outside as well as the inside. She didn't believe she was worth the effort of somebody else caring. She didn't feel worthy of the responses she received.

Maria's story may be different than yours or mine, however, her feelings are identifiable with most of us. Maria's makeover was not as much about her appearance rather, it was about how she felt about herself! Not being enough is an epidemic in our society. Have you ever told anybody that they are enough just as they are? If not, I encourage you to express this to somebody that you know! Watch how uncomfortable yet grateful they feel. I have brought people to tears, even grown men, by telling them they are enough and worthy of more, worthy of love, acceptance, and success.

Do you want to take steps to feel you are enough? As you are reading this chapter do you see where the feelings of inadequacy stop you from living your authentic self? Follow the exercises below to begin changing your mindset. Living a true life with a voice and a purpose means realizing your worth!

# For Reflection

What happened in your life that created this belief? Was there somebody in your life that told you that you were not enough? Was there an incident that resonates in you creating this belief? Were you teased or bullied in school? Has there been a significant other that has mentally, emotionally, or physically hurt you? Take a moment and write it all down. It is important for you to first identify that you feel you are not enough but then to also uncover why, in order to proceed with changing your mindset.

_____

_____

_____

_____

_____

_____

_____

_____

_____

_____

_____

_____

_____

_____

_____

_____

_____

*Finding Your Voice*

The way to change your mindset is to first get real about who you are, what you want, and how you feel. Next, I want you to look in the mirror and identify attributes about yourself physically and emotionally that you like. Write them all down. This is an important step in your process.

# *Attributes*
## THAT I LIKE ABOUT MYSELF

_____     _____
_____     _____
_____     _____
_____     _____
_____     _____
_____     _____
_____     _____
_____     _____
_____     _____
_____     _____
_____     _____
_____     _____
_____     _____
_____     _____
_____     _____
_____     _____
_____     _____
_____     _____
_____     _____

Once the list is complete, I want you to identify who you want to be but maybe aren't quite there yet. Once you have created both lists, combine them together and create sentences that begin with "I am". Below are examples:

" I am beautiful inside and out."

"I am funny."

"I am adventurous."

"I am intelligent."

"I am loyal."

"I am kind."

"I am forgiving. "

"I am successful."

"I am a good mom."

"I am a good wife."

After you have created the list of "I am" read through them. Look in the mirror and say them to yourself. The very last "I am" should say "I am enough just as I am." You need to repeat this list to yourself in the morning before you leave the house, and at night before you go to bed. What do you believe will happen if you do this exercise twice a day for 30 days? You will begin to believe it! I had Maria do this very exercise! I am proud to report that Maria's feelings about herself began to shift. Whenever Maria begins doubting herself, I have her pull out her list. Maria has become a confident woman who believes in herself and realizes she is enough, just as she is! She went on to take a key position in my company and is also a very special friend in my life. I am proud of her daily for her growth!

# CHAPTER SIX

# The Victim vs. Survivor Mentality

## "IT'S A CHOICE"

Have you met those people that are unhappy with their life and love to talk about it? We all have friends and acquaintances that when asked how they are, they burst into negativity in regard to their circumstances. Whether it be their career, their relationships, their children -- really anything -- they just want to complain. They may even take it a step further and ask you for your advice but then tell you all the reasons why your advice won't work or that they have tried it before.

On the flip side, have you met the person that always has a smile on their face and seems genuinely happy most of the time? It doesn't matter what you ask them, their response seems positive and uplifting. They rarely seem upset and if they do, it's short lived and doesn't stand in their way of moving forward. Do you ever look at this person and long for what they have?

I met a middle-aged woman recently whom we'll call Irene. Her story brings to light just how much being a victim, or a survivor is a choice. Irene was in an arranged marriage for most of her life. She raised three beautiful children who grew up to be doctors just like their father. Irene's husband was a highly esteemed doctor in their city. Her family chose him for her because they knew he would be an adequate provider for their daughter. He came from a well-rounded, well established family. Living in America, to the outside world, Irene had it all! She had her children, lived in a large beautiful home, had fancy cars, social engagements, fundraisers, and all the bells and whistles of a wealthy family. What people didn't see behind closed doors was the loveless empty marriage, infidelity, and abuse.

Irene decided early on in her relationship that she was going to make the best of her situation. She started working when the children were old enough and in school. She went to college and received several degrees. Irene ended up in a lucrative position in the medical field. Many women in her culture stayed repressed and controlled but Irene kept moving forward no matter what the circumstances of her homelife were.

Irene had a defining moment that changed the course of her life. Her husband became physically abusive with her one day, and something snapped inside of her. She decided in that moment to call the police knowing full well there was no going back from her decision. After the police came, she called her grown children to let them know she was finished accepting this life as it was. She then called her parents to confirm her decision to leave the marriage. In spite of their culture and fear of persecution from friends and family, her parents agreed to help her end the marriage and file for divorce. Irene was able to break free from the repression of her marriage and chose the life she wanted to live regardless of what those around her said.

Irene was able to split the assets in the divorce, had her degrees and her career, and was able to set up an entirely new life full of excitement and relief. She no longer had to wear a fake smile or pretend that everything was okay. Her world was opened up to pure freedom for the first time in her life!

When I asked Irene about her defining moment and the choice she made, she made it clear that she would not change the life she had or the choices she made when the time was right. Irene never chose to be a victim of her circumstances. She chose to rise above, better herself, and prepare for the next phase of her life.

There are many women living the life that Irene lived. They feel they don't have a choice and can never break free from their circumstances. Whether it be because of money, lifestyle, survival, or relational, these women are paralyzed inside and "stuck" where they are. They can't find the strength within themselves, so they stay a victim of their circumstances. They tend to look at the worst-case scenario when really, they need to ask themselves one question;

## "What's the best that can happen?"

The hardest part of life can sometimes be the choice between being a victim or being a survivor. It does not matter what your childhood looked like; whether you had abuse, neglect, or maybe you were bullied. My brother and I are nine years apart and our lives were very different, although we grew up in the same family. I shared with you previously that I experienced mental, physical, and sexual abuse at an early age, and that my mother was an addict, so I basically raised myself for much of my childhood.

By the time my brother came along, things were beginning to change. Our mother started getting her life together in his toddler years. My mom married an amazing man and my parents started going to church. My mom was clean and sober by the time my brother was four. He grew up in a loving family with parents that were home and participants in his life. For me, the "damage" as some would call it, had been done.

In High School, I began going to a school counselor a couple of times a week. I realized I had anger issues and was having a hard time coping with the abuse that occurred. I chose not to be a victim of my circumstances, rather I decided to deal with them head on. I was able to forgive my abusers and see the bigger picture – the behind the scenes story of their life -- that led to them becoming how they were. Most importantly, I recognized I was chosen for this path and there were lessons to be learned and strength to be gained. I rose above the pain that paralyzed me and drew strength from it.

My brother chose a different path. He became a meth addict at fourteen. For years, he felt entitled in life and that he deserved concessions. My brother stayed an addict for over ten years until one day he realized enough was enough. He gained back control of his life through his faith and changed from being a victim of his circumstances to being a survivor. He took ownership for his life and choices. That is the beauty of our journey, we can change our mindset and our path at any time! We are never truly "stuck" except maybe in our own mind.

# For Reflection

It is time to check yourself. Are you a victim or a survivor? In this exercise, I'd like you to make a list of all the circumstances you believe others have created in your life, and think about what you learned about yourself as a result of that circumstance. Then list the things you are grateful for. There are things to be grateful for and lessons to be learned in all scenarios of our life. Accepting what has happened, embracing the experience, and realizing you would not be who you are today had you not gone through them, is the key to finding your true voice. Accept each circumstance and write out all of the things you have become because of the experience.

Circumstance created:

_____
_____
_____
_____

_____
_____
_____
_____

_____
_____
_____
_____

I learned about myself that:

_____

_____

_____

_____

_____

_____

_____

_____

_____

_____

_____

_____

I'm grateful for/that:

_____

_____

_____

_____

_____

_____

_____

_____

_____

_____

_____

Would you change it after reviewing the traits the circumstances helped you develop? You are ready for the next step!

# CHAPTER SEVEN

# Setting Boundaries

W hy is it that most of us have an inability to say no when we don't want to do something? It is because women are innately created to nurture, and our natural instinct is to take care of anything that is asked of us. The real question is; by saying no, are we being selfish? Does it make us selfish to practice self-care and self-management? No! If we do not first take care of ourselves, we cannot truly take care of others the way we desire.

I used to have a real problem with saying no. In my previous marriage, it seemed the only way to keep the peace was to be a yes girl. I wore myself out! Every morning my husband wanted a full cooked breakfast with eggs, sausage, and hash browns. He ate several times a day and refused to make anything for himself. It didn't matter if I worked a twelve-hour day in the field, he would wait until I got home and then ask, "what are you making for dinner?" I, being the dutiful wife, no matter how tired I was, would then make dinner, even if it was ten o'clock at night. I grew bitter because I was running my real estate business, keeping up with the

house, and cooking for him morning and night. His life consisted of going to the gym for a couple of hours, eating the breakfast he expected when he got home, meandering around for a couple of hours playing on his phone, having lunch or a meeting out that never seemed to bring in business, and then would go drink with his buddies for a few hours before coming home for dinner and going to sleep after eating. No, he was not always this way. He evolved over time into this type of man.

I started going to counseling to deal with my frustrations and bitterness that were growing inside. My counselor helped me realize I created the world I lived in because of my inability to say no. I was not setting boundaries to practice self-care and self-management. I wasn't making myself a priority and I was beginning to burn out.

It was difficult for me to accept that I had created the expectations placed on me by allowing the requests and never taking a stand for myself. People, no matter who they are, will treat you how you allow them to treat you. Through counseling, I learned how to practice self-care and self-management and began saying no. I had to come to terms with the fact that this did not make me selfish. It was necessary for me to find my voice and exercise what was best for me. I would love to tell you my husband was supportive of the change. Unfortunately, he could not accept that I needed to be taken care of as well. It became abundantly clear that my husband was a "what's in it for me" type of person and my needs were not important to him.

When we start practicing self-care and self-management, the natural evolution of our current relationships will change. Those that are takers in your life will begin to disappear because you are not fulfilling their need of you to the detriment of yourself. Those that truly love you and care about you will see the changes as a positive step for you because their concern is your wellbeing. You may be afraid of this weeding out process, but I can promise you it will be one of your most important steps in your growth of finding your voice.

What does self-care and self-management mean? It means that when you are tired, you take a break because your body requires it. It means saying no if it's your day off and you need to rest. Taking time to go to the gym and not allowing anything to get in the way of that. Asking for help when you need it. Let's say that again.... asking for help when you need it! Asking for help is a large request for most of us because we feel we should be able to handle it all on our own. Why do we feel that way? Is there a rule book somewhere that says we are supposed to be able to handle everything on our own and never need help from anybody? Why do we feel guilty if we ask the kids or our husband to help us with dinner? This is a limiting belief that must come out of your mind! Self-care and self-management means asking for help when you need it and not feeling bad about it.

**It is okay to say NO!**

Recently I was speaking with a very dear friend of mine,

Jackie. For years her desire has been to serve others. Jackie has been on a path of finding her authentic self for a couple of years and she hit a wall of realization recently. She had been sacrificing herself and her ambitions to satisfy others, including her husband.

As Jackie began chasing her ambitions, her marriage started struggling. Her husband wanted her to stay home and take care of their home, the children and his needs. Jackie's heart had always been to serve others on a larger scale than just those at home. The thought of not pursuing her ambitions, and what she believed to be her purpose was suffocating. She grew bitter and frustrated as she felt repressed by her husband's limiting beliefs of her worth.

Jackie began pushing back, which created an uncomfortable transition in her relationships with others. She began defining what she wanted her world to look like and how to take action. Jackie started communicating her feelings instead of holding them inside. She began stating when situations or comments did not feel good to her. She and her husband separated for a period of time to determine if her vision and his could come together in unity.

While separated, Jackie and her husband began counseling separately and together. They unveiled several truths about who they were as people and the boxes they had placed themselves into throughout the marriage. Both were able to articulate what was important to them and what was not acceptable. Jackie began scheduling things that were important for her growth. Her husband began accepting his part in the broken relationship and was willing to make changes to support Jackie. They were able to come back together through owning their part in what had occurred in the marriage. One of the hardest realizations for Jackie was the fact that she had been treated how she had allowed others to treat her. This has been a process of revelation for Jackie and her husband and one that will continue as they rediscover and redefine their relationship and their roles in their marriage and household.

How can we expect others to know what we need if we do not articulate what is important to us? Setting boundaries and learning to say no is the beginning of building a life surrounded by those that honor and respect us. At first, your fears will be other's reactions. You do not have control over other people and how they feel. You only have control over you. You cannot be afraid of losing people because those that want to only take from you are not worthy to be in your life. It will become abundantly clear who those people are around you that are in it for themselves. You are better off to let them go.

Sadly, my husband was not able, nor did he choose to accept that I was not at his beck and call. He was one of the few that were in my life because of what I provided for him. Yes, it was painful to realize my needs were not important to him. It was even more painful to realize I had allowed him to devalue me because I had not placed value in myself.

As I continued setting boundaries for myself, his selfishness became clear and I had to say good-bye. I had to value myself and recognize that I was enough just as I was and worthy of somebody loving me for me, not what I could do for them. Although it was a difficult decision, my life moving forward turned out better because I was willing to value myself. I can promise myself and you one thing; I will never allow myself to be devalued again. My hope is that you will take the same stand for yourself by practicing self-care and self-management!

# For Reflection

Write down a list of all the things you do for other people and how you feel about them.

_____
_____
_____
_____
_____
_____
_____
_____
_____
_____
_____
_____
_____
_____

Are there things on your list that frustrate you or make you feel bitter?

_____
_____
_____
_____
_____
_____
_____

Why do these specific things bother you?

_____
_____
_____
_____
_____
_____
_____
_____

Are there things that others in your life can be responsible for?

_____
_____
_____
_____
_____
_____
_____

# Exercise #1

On a calendar:

1. write down in black ink what you do for everybody else on a daily basis.

2. In red ink, write down what you do for yourself. (Recognize that the black ink more than likely outweighs the red ink.)

3. Find areas where you can add in more red ink time for things you enjoy.

4. Begin adding those items to your future calendar.

# Exercise #2

Identify people in your life whom the relationship seems one sided.

_____

_____

_____

_____

_____

Write down what you would like to be different in how you are being treated.

_____

_____

_____

_____

_____

_____

1. Construct a bullet point conversation you would like to have with these people individually in order for them to understand your needs and desires.

•

•

•

•

•

•

•

•

•

•

•

•

•

•

•

Remember, when you have the conversation, you are not in control of their responses, you are only in control of you. When having these conversations, it is important to state what you value about them in your life before you state what you would like to change. People respond better with a positive prior to a negative.

2. Schedule time for your conversation to take place. If the person you are having the conversation with is a male, make sure they are able to focus only on the conversation and are not in the middle of anything else.

3. Read over your "I am" list from chapter five. List the areas of your life that you would like more respect for who you really are.

_____
_____
_____
_____
_____
_____
_____
_____
_____
_____
_____
_____
_____

Recognize the value behind your "I am" statements and how important they are to you.

Begin keeping the "I am" statements always close to you through the setting boundaries process. Read them regularly. This enables a belief system in you about yourself that provides a platform of how others view you.

4. Recite to yourself daily the following statement:

"I AM ENOUGH JUST AS I AM.

MY LIFE HAS VALUE.

I HAVE VALUE.

MY NEEDS AND DESIRES MATTER.

I AM WORTHY OF LOVE FROM
MYSELF AND OTHERS.

IT IS OKAY FOR ME TO PRACTICE
SELF-CARE AND SELF-MANAGEMENT."

# CHAPTER EIGHT

# Forgiveness

Forgiveness can be tricky. Sometimes we say we have forgiven someone but in reality, we still harbor the pain of the experience. How does one truly forgive? Forgiveness is not for the weak of heart. Forgiveness takes a strength and understanding beyond what most are taught. In this chapter, you will find a strategy for forgiving others and also yourself.

Have you ever looked at the whole person that has hurt you? What I mean is, have you pieced together their whole picture of life and pondered why they do the things they do? One of the biggest issues with forgiveness and the pain others have caused us is that we take things so personal. This is going to be a hard pill to swallow but you need to hear it and understand it. The majority of the time, in fact, ninety-nine percent of the time, their actions are not personal and have nothing to do with us!

People act in different ways and respond based on the lives they have lived, their upbringing, their circumstances, and their experiences in life. People act based on what they know, how they grew up, and experiences they have had. Most people have survival mechanisms they have built over time that begin to define who they are and how they treat others. The story below gives a good understanding of the process of forgiveness.

Remember the story I shared with you about my cousin who molested me from the ages of four through seven? When I was about fifteen years old, that same cousin came to live at our house for a short period of time. At first, I was angry and hurt that my parents allowed him to come live with us. I was terrified at the thought of him being in my home. I had to process my anger and fear and decided I could either be a victim of the situation or I could face it head on and choose to be a survivor. In doing so, I began to realize that my parents didn't know the magnitude of what had occurred when I was younger. I had never shared the details or for just how long the molestation happened. I then started to see the bigger picture of my cousin, who had been tormented his entire life.

As my cousin arrived, I saw a broken down and beaten man. He had become an addict and sold himself on the streets to whomever would pay the price for his drugs. He was severely underweight, and his face was sunken in to a skeletal form. He was at our house to try and recover and as I watched him, I couldn't help but feel sadness for the man standing before me.

My cousin grew up in an abusive home where he was treated by his stepfather like he was worthless and insignificant.

71

I remember watching him go through the abuse of having his hair shaved off because he got in trouble at school. His mouth was duct taped shut several times. He was kicked in his stomach and his back on several occasions. The circumstances of his life growing up clearly had a devastating effect on who he became. Most would say this was sweet justice for what he did to me as a child. I, on the other hand, decided that nobody should have to endure what this man had in his adolescent years.

One evening, after everybody went to bed, my cousin was sitting in the living room by himself. I decided to take this opportunity to confront him on what he did to me as a child. I sat down on the couch next to him and turned to face him. While sitting next to him, I could feel his shame and guilt had taken over. He had a hard time looking me in the eyes. I was extremely nervous but was determined we were going to discuss what happened and how he violated me. I wasn't sure what my objective was but knew I had to get it out of me!

I began the conversation with a caring tone and explained I wanted to understand some things. As I began talking gently, his eyes began to meet mine. I asked him why he did those bad things to me and explained that I needed to understand so I could let it go. His eyes filled with tears as he explained that he did to me what had been done to him.

He cried as he explained I was not the only one he had hurt and had spent his life with regret for the things he had done to others. He apologized for hurting me and said he wished he could take it back. He sobbed as he spoke the words and I just sat quietly and listened, tears streaming down my face. My cousin was a product of his environment and what he knew. He had spent the rest of his life up to this point punishing himself through drugs and allowing others to continually hurt him in hopes it would compensate for the pain he had caused others.

Overwhelming sadness and compassion came over me as I spoke the words, "I forgive you" and a release came over me in that moment, at the young age of fifteen. I faced my abuser, confronted him, and was able to tell him I forgave him, and more importantly, I meant it. I saw a glimmer of hope in him as I explained that God could forgive him for all things he had done in his life. I shared God's love with him and explained that I could forgive him because of the love God showed me through Christ. I told my cousin about all the things I saw happen to him while he was growing up and I understood that he was a product of his circumstances. He asked if he could hug me and thanked me for not hating him. He made a promise to continue seeking help and would not hurt others anymore. He lived his promise until the end. He left my house a few days later but stayed in contact with my parents. My cousin died about seven years later of AIDS. He had contracted the deadly virus during the time when he allowed others to punish him. I am thankful for that night because he and I were both set free.

Many have asked over the years how I could forgive

such a horrible crime against me. It is not about the offense as much as it is being able to take ourselves out of it. I was able to realize the offense had nothing to do with me personally. It was about the issues my cousin had. He would've done that to someone, even if it wasn't me. The only thing you can do is see the other person for who they are, and how they got there. Here's another example of how understanding the bigger picture allows for the ability to forgive.

Linda was in a difficult relationship with George. She asked herself over and over again why she continued to love this man that would be amazing for a while and then seemingly hit the self-destruct button. George battled drug and alcohol addiction but seemed to really want a different life. Along with his alcohol and drug addictions he would say inappropriate things to other women, and this deeply hurt Linda. Even though Linda was pretty, intelligent, and had a fierce passion, Linda felt she was not enough or George would not be compelled to do all of these things.

George, recognizing he was going to lose Linda, stepped up his game and got help. He became clean and sober, helped Linda with her business, and refrained from inappropriate contact with other women. George worked really hard for quite some time on himself and gained the respect of Linda because of his determination. Linda felt George had truly grown and become the man she always knew he could be. Because of the significant changes in George, Linda agreed to marry him.

For the first several months, Linda was the happiest she had ever been in her life. George was an amazing husband and seemed so happy! The couple made love every day, worked together, had an amazing time going on dates and spending quality time together. Linda never wanted to lose this feeling of love and pure joy. George was glowing with happiness as well. Others made comments all the time that they had never seen a man so happy to be married. Life was fantastic and everything Linda hoped it would be.

About eight months into the marriage, George went to the bar and had a few drinks. The couple had been arguing that day and George used the arguing as an excuse to drink. When he came home, Linda was crushed. On top of the drinking, George proceeded to tell her about a woman he met at the bar that wanted to take him home with her. Linda felt so sick inside and hurt that she had ever committed herself to him. All of the flashbacks of other incidents began running through her head. Linda knew in that moment that her loving and passionate George had just left and may never return because his demons had returned.

Over the next several months, George began drinking from morning until bed. He was also high all the time on marijuana. His porn addiction kicked into full gear as well. Sometimes he would be on twenty-six or more sites a day. Linda felt like if she were "enough" for her husband, who she loved dearly, he would not need any of these vices. In her mind, the problem must be her! George didn't hesitate to reiterate that to her on a regular basis as well. This all felt so personal to her. How could George do this to her? Why would he hurt her this way?

Sadly, George only continued to get worse and his self-destructive behavior became present in full force. He eventually cheated on Linda. When the woman called her, Linda's switch inside of herself flipped and she knew it was time to say good-bye to George. They were at a point of no return. The George she loved with all her heart was never going to come back.

Linda felt such an anger growing inside herself. How could this man intentionally hurt her this way? It felt so personal and her heart was shattered. One thing Linda had on her side was a survivor mentality! She refused to be a victim of her circumstances. Linda realized she needed to be grateful for the lessons learned and she needed to find a way to forgive George, not because she wanted him back but because it was best for her to move forward.

Linda began looking at the bigger picture of George. What type of family did he grow up in? What disappointments had George experienced in his life? How did he become an addict? Why did he have such a disregard and lack of respect for women? She began piecing together George's life with everything she knew about him.

George grew up in a family that had few happy moments. His father was a womanizer and had many affairs while George was growing up. His father's belief was that the wife should take care of the family and him while he was out conquering women that were meant for fun and sleeping with. George's mother was a kind-hearted person that grew up in foster care and was separated from her siblings. She accepted the life with George's father in order to keep her family together; however, she was a very bitter woman because of her loveless marriage. George began drinking and dabbling in drugs at the age of fifteen.

At seventeen, I feel it is too detailed and could tell people who know the story who this is. Replace with: There was a horrible incident between George and his father that devastated George. After the incident, George shut down all emotions and heavily went into drug use and alcohol. George continued on this path and following the footsteps of his father with women.

As Linda pieced together George's life, she was able to realize that George's actions while in her life were not personal, rather they were the actions of a broken man who was acting on what he knew. Because of her love for George, yes, she was shattered; however, she was able to forgive him and set her broken heart free. She was ready to move forward, learn from her experiences, be grateful for the lessons, and recognize how strong the experience had made her.

I know this is an extreme story, which is why I'm sharing it with you. If Linda could forgive George for things that were so huge and seemed so personal, it should be easy to see how one could forgive for much less of an offense. We cannot move forward with our life, dreams, and goals unless we first learn how to forgive others and not take things so personal. One of the hardest lessons in forgiveness is how to forgive ourselves.

Linda is another great example of learning to forgive yourself. Linda is a strong businesswoman. People look up to her, and she seems to have a good head on her shoulders. So, if all of this is true, how could she let somebody like George penetrate her world? How could she fall in love with somebody so broken? Linda found herself angrier with herself than with George. She felt she couldn't trust herself or her judgment when it came to men. Truthfully, she felt completely stupid for marrying him!

Linda had to take a step back and look at her own life and circumstances. Linda grew up in a family of addiction where erratic and unpredictable behavior became normal to her. Although she swore she would never get involved with an addict, she saw something amazing in George that allowed her to put the red flags to the back of her mind.

Linda's family had all recovered over the years. Linda had to come to terms with the fact that she tried to save George because she had an undying, unwavering hope for George because of her family's recovery history. Linda had to forgive herself for not being able to change George or love him enough for him to make better choices for himself and their family. In counseling, Linda learned that an addict's choices had to be theirs and she could not control the outcome. Unfortunately, most addicts never recover, no matter how much they are loved.

Because of looking at the bigger picture of her own life, Linda was able to forgive herself just as much as she was able to forgive George. Ironically, the forgiveness of herself was more challenging. The biggest part of forgiveness is that it is not for the benefit of the other person, it is for you. You cannot move forward with your life fully until you look at these things and

1. Accept what has occurred.

2. Accept the lessons you have learned.

3. Be grateful for the experience.

4. Look at the bigger picture of the other person and forgive them.

5. Look at the bigger picture of yourself and forgive you.

6. Remember, it is not personal!

Forgiveness of yourself and others will set you free to live a life of having your voice and fulfilling your purpose. Harboring hurt feelings and obsessing over what others have done to you will only hold you back from being the best version of you. The exercises below will walk you through how to forgive others and yourself so that you can be free from the burdens of your past and move forward to your future. This can be one of the most painful steps, but as I've said before, with pain comes growth.

# *For Reflection*

Now that you understand how to forgive, think of the different experiences in your life that you still have not forgiven. On the pages that follow, write each experience on a separate page. If you need more space then what has been provided, write them on a separate sheet of paper.

• Look at each experience and ponder the person that hurt you.

• Look at the bigger picture of the person and events that occurred. Write it all out.

• Look at the bigger picture of you, your actions, and how you allowed something like this into your life. Write it all down.

# I HAVE NOT FORGIVEN:

---
---
---

# WHAT HAPPENED:

---
---
---
---
---
---
---
---
---
---
---
---
---
---
---
---
---
---
---
---
---
---
---

# THE BIG PICTURE OF THIS IS:

_____
_____
_____
_____
_____
_____
_____
_____
_____
_____
_____
_____
_____
_____
_____
_____
_____
_____
_____
_____
_____
_____
_____
_____
_____
_____
_____
_____
_____
_____

# I HAVE NOT FORGIVEN:

_____

_____

_____

_____

# WHAT HAPPENED:

_____

_____

_____

_____

_____

_____

_____

_____

_____

_____

_____

_____

_____

_____

_____

_____

_____

_____

_____

_____

_____

_____

# THE BIG PICTURE OF THIS IS:

_____
_____
_____
_____
_____
_____
_____
_____
_____
_____
_____
_____
_____
_____
_____
_____
_____
_____
_____
_____
_____
_____
_____
_____
_____
_____
_____
_____

After you have gone through the above steps:

1. Write down the names of all people that have hurt you in the past that you need to be set free from on separate small pieces of paper. ( Include your name on one of the pieces of paper as well.)

2. Burn each name individually as you say "_____ (their name) you no longer have power over my life. I see your bigger picture and I forgive you."

*WHEN YOU COME TO YOUR NAME, SAY THE WORDS"_____ (YOUR NAME) I UNDERSTAND YOUR BIGGER PICTURE AND I RELEASE YOU FROM HARBORED PAIN, I FORGIVE YOU _____ (YOUR NAME) AND I LOVE YOU. YOU ARE ENOUGH."*

You should feel an instant release, but this exercise does not stop old feelings from coming up occasionally. When those feelings arise in you, go back in your mind to burning their name and forgiving them. Always remember the words:

**"You have no power over me."**

Over time, the feelings will come less and less to eventually not at all. You are now free to move forward on your journey!

CHAPTER NINE

# Relationships with Men

You have read my story and I am sure you can understand that having a good relationship with men has been one of my biggest challenges. I have learned that understanding men and how they think is a great help. I made it a goal not just to understand them, but embrace them. So many times, men's actions baffle us because we were created to act and think differently.

Because of the pain I experienced as a child at the hand of different boys and men in my life, I had formed a limiting belief that men could not be trusted. I didn't realize this limiting belief existed until I started recalling relationships with men throughout my life.

There is an amazing book called "The Queen's Code" written by Alison A. Armstrong. Armstrong illustrates in this book through different characters, the differences between how men and women think and act. As my friends and I read through the book, it became quite clear to us that women emasculate men in ways we don't even realize. I was so taken with this book, I began sending apologies to exes for the different ways I could see I emasculated them and didn't realize it at the time.

We sadly live in a world where "ball busting" has become socially acceptable and the norm. It is all around us on TV, movies, and interaction in public. What if men are not the actual problem? What if men were allowed to be who they are meant to be and not continuously stripped of their manhood?

Do I believe that men should "rule" over you? Absolutely not! I would never suggest such a thing, especially with gaining my voice as a female. But what if there is the possibility of having a mutually respecting relationship where both the man and woman were able to be who they are meant to be? What if you could have it all? I believe you can!

Men have an innate desire to be providers and protectors. Just recently I was at dinner and overheard a woman say to the man she was with, "If you made more money, I could order the filet mignon and not have to share dinner with you." I watched as his shoulders slumped inward and I could see the feeling of "failing" come over his face. He didn't say much after that. When they finished their meal, he offered to put on her jacket for her. He had a beaming smile. She grabbed the jacket out of his hands and said she could do it herself. Again, I watched as his shoulders hunched inward, eyes went to the floor, and he walked out not even trying to hold the door for her.

How many times have we had conversations like this

with the men in our lives? Maybe they didn't help at home, forgot to take out the trash, left their dishes everywhere? Maybe we were frustrated, and it came out in ways that crushed them? Women have no idea the power they have over men. We have the ability to crush them in moments, which may give us satisfaction for a moment but then what? We get upset when they start losing interest in us. Maybe they don't want to be intimate or help us with anything? They suddenly become busy and stop spending quality time with us. We as women then become more ruthless, trying to strip their manhood even more only to push them further away. What a vicious cycle!

Let me ask you this; have you been in relationships where everything starts out great and then things change? He begins by making an effort to schedule dates with you, conversation seems to flow, intimacy seems to be going well, and you fall head over heels in love with him? All of a sudden, he starts pulling back, maybe after an argument or a conversation? Our immediate response is to push, blame him, get angry and have thoughts of "Oh here we go again! Another one, afraid of commitment! Men suck!" Does this sound familiar? Is it possible that you were emasculating him and didn't realize it because it has become so "normal" to you?

Let me enlighten you. Men feel emasculated by some of what we might consider "small" things. Let's say we are in a conversation with a man and we keep interrupting them when they speak. Eventually they just stop talking! Have you noticed that? Their mind goes to "They don't really care what I have to say so why say anything?" Men take great pride in providing. If we mention anything about lack of something we need that they provide, it is a direct slap to their face. Men are naturally protectors. Be prepared that if you mention anything that they need to protect you from, they will go into protect mode. If you don't allow them to help, they will feel emasculated. This goes for anything we need help with by the way! If a man offers his help and we turn him down, we are emasculating him!

I used to say something to my ex-husband that I didn't see anything wrong with. I would say, "I am with you because I choose to be, not because I need you." To me, I wanted to prove that I could take care of myself. What I didn't realize is that in giving myself this power, I stripped him of his. I took his balls right off in that statement. Men need to feel needed and cherished just as much as we do.

Women have been taught to be self-sufficient, take care of themselves, and not be needy. I am not proposing that we become helpless and damsels in distress. I am proposing that if we want true and real relationships with men in our lives, whether it be working relationships, friendship, or romantic relationships, we learn to accept who they are and how they think. It is not fair to compare them to women because they are not us and are not meant to be. The world has been created and evolved over time because of the efforts of both men and women. Our world does not function without the existence of both and the gifts and thought processes we both bring to the table. They desire to be with us just as much as we desire to be with them. We both want to be appreciated and accepted for who we are meant to be. There is a special dance that is created between a man and a woman who understand one another.

After learning the differences between men and women and how we think and feel differently, I have laid down my power to castrate men. I have a new perspective on men and an appreciation for who they are. I cherish my male friendships and working relationships in a whole new light. I ask them questions when I do not understand their thought process and actually wait for them to finish their thoughts. I am amazed at how willing they are to help with things. How attentive they are when I speak. My safety and security have become their top priority even just as friends. I am looked at in a whole new light because I have decided to allow them to be who they innately are and chose to understand them better.

Your relationship with men can be very rewarding to both you and them. It is time to lay down your power to castrate them and learn to embrace the unique qualities men can add to your life. My hope is that you will work through the exercises below and find the importance of men in your balance of life and love.

# *For Reflection*

If you would like a different and rewarding relationship with men, go through the following exercises

1. Think back on your relationships with men over your lifetime. Have there been relationships that were harmful to you and have made you feel you cannot trust men? Write them down and be honest how it made you feel.

_____

_____

_____

_____

_____

_____

What has been your preconceived ideas about men because of things you have heard or experienced that you may be wrong about?

_____

_____

_____

_____

_____

What decisions have you made regarding your relationships with men moving forward in your life after reading this chapter?

_____

_____

_____

_____

_____

_____

_____

How has your current relationships with men been going for you? Are you content with your current male relationships or are you constantly feeling frustrated and let down?

_____

_____

_____

_____

_____

_____

_____

_____

_____

_____

_____

2. What is the"perfect image" that you have created in your mind that a man should be?  Write your list.

_____
_____
_____
_____
_____
_____
_____
_____
_____
_____
_____
_____
_____
_____

Is your list realistic or are you expecting men to be "women" in your life

_____

3. What type of relationship would you truly prefer to have with a man?  Write it out.

_____
_____
_____
_____
_____

Is it possible to have this type of relationship?

_____

-Are there things you need to change about yourself in order to allow this type of relationship?  (It's important to get real with yourself on this!)

_____
_____
_____
_____
_____

Recommended Reading:

The Queen's Code by Alison A. Armstrong to begin your new journey of relationships with men!

CHAPTER TEN

# Sensual Feminine Power

T his is by far one of my favorite topics to speak and
teach about. Women get so caught up in filling roles
and trying to be the perfect woman on the outside,
they tend to forget who they are on the inside. Women crave
to be sensual beings but become inhibited by fear of rejection
and judgement. There is a difference between sensual and
sexual, although they do go hand in hand. This chapter is not
for the faint or prude of heart. If you are repressing who you
are behind closed doors because of your fears, keep reading! If
you are completely satisfied with your sex life and do not feel
inhibited in any way, you may not need to read this chapter...
unless you are curious.

Women have been taught to satisfy their men in hopes
the men will not go elsewhere. Then why are the statistics of
women cheating on the rise? Is it possible that women are
not getting what we need and desire? Women must feel an
emotional connection in most cases in order to be sensual.
We all have the ability to be sexual but what does sensual

mean? In the Merriam Webster dictionary, the definition of sensual means; "relating to or consisting in the gratification of the senses or the indulgence of appetite." What does this really mean, indulging in other things that stimulate your senses other than intercourse? When women are stimulated through all of their senses, they become sensual beings that ooze sexuality!

Remember in the previous chapter "Relationships with Men", we discussed men's desire to provide. Well I am about to blow your mind ladies! Men's desire to provide even stems in the bedroom. Their desire is to give you pleasure. Yes, you heard me! If that is not happening in your bedroom, two things are going on. You are not articulating what you want and desire, and he is feeling like he's failing you. This is when the bedroom becomes dull and almost scripted.

Recently I was speaking with a woman who had been married for fifteen plus years. Her sex life with her husband had been scheduled twice a week for most of their marriage. She was starting to feel like sex in their marriage had become a chore to both of them and had lost the romance and intimacy. As she blushed while I asked her questions, she admitted she had never told him what she liked or wanted to experience. They had never, in fifteen years, had a conversation about either of their desires. I noticed while we spoke that she felt very timid and shy. I could tell she certainly didn't feel sexy.

My question to her and to you is this; if you don't tap into your sexy, therefore sensual self, how can you expect your spouse or partner to? Sexy is an attitude, not a look. Sexy comes from within where you own your inner desires and know you own your man! Feeling sexy draws out the sensual power from within and draws your spouse or boyfriend to you because they can feel it. Owning who you are behind closed doors allows you to own your man!

I asked my friend several questions of things she has always wanted to do, how she wanted to feel, in order to give her an assignment. She had always wanted to initiate, not on a scheduled day, and was afraid to be rejected. This is a common fear ladies. Don't let it stop you! Her assignment: After the kids were in bed, she was to go to her bedroom and walk right up to her husband, give him "the look", and back him up to the wall passionately kissing him. She needed to have full confidence while undressing him even if he was shocked, which he would be. Her fantasy was to dominate the moment. He had always been the initiator. Her task was to dominate and please him while not allowing him to take over. She agreed reluctantly and promised not to run away from her assignment. My last questions to her was, "What's the best that could happen?" Her response, blushing, "I could blow his mind!"

The next day, she insisted on seeing me. As she walked in the room, she was glowing! She proceeded to tell me, without intimate detail, how nervous she was at first. She then tapped into her sensual feminine power, gained her sexy confidence and backed him right up against the wall. She said he literally melted with joy as she proceeded to live out her sensual fantasy with her husband. Afterward, he wanted another round! He was completely perplexed and elated at the change and wanted more.

Since her first assignment, she has started pondering other ideas and fantasies. She and her husband have had conversations without embarrassment of things they would both enjoy together. They still have their scheduled times to ensure they make time to please each other, however there are more times where spontaneity comes about. Because of her new found sensual feminine power, my friend walks with a different confidence in and out of the bedroom. She has taken steps to own who she is!

Owning who you are and what you want behind closed doors is essential to your fulfilling life. How can you own who you are in the world if you can't own who you are and articulate what your needs are to your loved one in the bedroom? The answer is, you can't! It is important to remember that sensual does not equal only sex just as sexy is an attitude not a look on the outside. Both come from within and are your right as a woman. You have the power inside of you to lose your inhibitions and become raw and naked with your significant other. What is the best that could happen? Your intimacy and sexual experiences reach all new heights together.

# For Reflection

Write out how you feel the most sensual through your senses.  What makes you feel sexy?

_____
_____
_____
_____
_____
_____
_____
_____
_____
_____
_____
_____
_____

What is a realistic fantasy that you have always wanted to try? Plan a time to make it happen.

_____
_____
_____
_____
_____

Set aside time to explore each other's bodies with your lover. The rule….it cannot end in actual intercourse, only foreplay. Make it even more fun by blindfolding each other as you each explore.

Begin conversations about what you both really enjoy or would like moving forward. Explore the possibilities together.

Remember, sensual does not equal sex even though it usually leads to sex. Sensual feminine power will unlock who you are in and out of the bedroom.

CHAPTER ELEVEN

# *The Evolution of You*

Throughout this book, I have shared my story as well as other women's stories of triumph over adversity. Through the exercises at the end of each chapter, you have been asked to identify different ways that your voice has been repressed. You have learned: who you are inside, you are enough just as you are, you have value, and hopefully have learned how to express to others what you need and desire. Most importantly, you have learned that you are not alone! To continue your growth of not only finding your voice, but also using it, you must seek out other likeminded women who choose to be survivors. Your growth and acceptance of yourself begins from within and will naturally spill over to those around you.

Others cannot accept us and love us the way we desire to be loved and accepted until we first love and accept ourselves. The ugly truths within us cannot be identified and worked through if we are not willing to do the work and forgive ourselves.

We all have things we need to change about ourselves and things we need to forgive others for as well. We deserve a life of meaning and purpose. By reading and going through the exercises in this book, you have begun your evolution of changing your patterns and practicing self-care and self-management.

Remember, change is a process and growth comes from pain. It has taken years to build the walls of "false protection" around you and it will take years to tear them down. Be easy on yourself and never give up on the pursuit to be the best version of you. Life is a journey of unexpected twists and turns. You now have the tools to navigate through your journey and never lose your footing on who you are. You are important! You are enough just as you are! You were created for greatness! You have now entered a world where your light can shine bright and your voice can be heard. You shall never accept anything less than you deserve again!

My hope is that you have grown through the process of reading this book and that my experiences as well as those of others have enlightened you and empowered you to move forward with your own voice. Life is an exciting journey of twists and turns. Our growth comes from navigating the twists and turns and growing from them. Thank you for taking this journey with me and for your willingness to grow.

# About the Author

Award-winning agent, author, speaker, and Real Estate Coach, Tina Valiant's journey to find her voice began over 20 years ago in Orlando, Florida where she went from being voted least likely to succeed to becoming the top sales agent in the company year after year, and then became known for her work in foreclosure defense, short sale negotiation, and loan modification -- negotiating over 1000 mortgage loans and helping hundreds of homeowners & investors save their property from foreclosure.

With over 17 years Real Estate experience, she now sells real estate in the Phoenix, Arizona market where The Arizona Journal of Real Estate & Business nominated her "Rookie of the Year" during her first year of sales. Since that time, her team, The TKay Group has become one of the top teams nationwide for the HomeSmart brand. Tina has earned a reputation throughout the country as an award winning team builder, and is passionate about coaching women who are seeking to take control of their lives and get free from the emotional and relational issues that block their success. Tina resides in Arizona, and has two adult daughters. This is her first book.

For more information on training with Tina, or to invite her to your event, visit www.TinaValiant.com.

# *Enjoyed this book?*

-- Women Thriving Together with Tina V --

https://www.facebook.com/groups/womenthrivingwithtinavaliant

Made in the USA
Columbia, SC
22 September 2024